MW00713551

My mother was an eternal optimist and she had a great influence on me. At each stage, she saw to it that I had a goal and a purpose for achieving my personal successes. What a joy to wake up every morning with a goal. There were often difficult challenges, but my attitude was always "Let's climb this hill and face the challenges with energy." Mark's book is a must-read for anyone facing a new phase of his or her life. I wholeheartedly embrace his wisdom and insights. Read this book!
Tom Van Arsdale, three-time NBA All-Star, businessman, author

This book is packed with facts, examples, and simple tips for taking control of your life. The best parts are the practical action plans which will drive the change you want to be. I highly recommend this book if you seek a new start.
Roy Newey, author, *Ready, Set, Grow!*

Mark once again packs twenty-two valuable, quick-hitting mentoring sessions into a very accessible format. Just what we need as we adjust to our new normal. Thanks Mark!
Timothy J, Brink, CEO, MCAA

If you are unhappy with your life and want to make changes, you've found the right book! Do what Mark asks you to do. Answer the questions at the end of each chapter. You will get to the place you want to go. I've done what Mark recommends and it works!

Ruth King, author, *The Courage to Be Profitable: Get and Stay Profitable in Less than 30 Minutes a Month*

Mark does it again! He combines the timeless success principles of all the greats into one easy read and he encourages you to act. Everyone who reads this book will not only improve their own life, but the lives of those around them.

Bob Logan, president, Plumbline Heating and Cooling

We can accept the current reality, or we can create it yourself. This short book is filled to the brim with proven advice and plans for accomplishing the latter.

Clay Moyle, author, *Sam Langford: Boxing's Greatest Uncrowned Champion*

As We THINK So We BECOME *is the book that ties all this "mind stuff" together. If great results are what you want, you're going to get them a-plenty in this book!*

Anthony Raymond, publisher, Kallisti Publishing

Mark always seems to hit life, and us, with a brick. His words of wisdom always unlock those things we need to do to enrich our lives and those of others. Keep them coming, Mark! We need your great stories and inspiration.

Ron Collier, PhD, business consultant, and author, *Profit Is an Attitude*

Mark Matteson is living proof of the power of positive thinking. He is among the most disciplined goal-setters and goal-achievers I know. His amazing accomplishments in basketball, sales, speaking, and publishing are proof that his method of using positive imagery to set goals, remain motivated, and work toward achieving goals really works. I'm excited to see what he accomplishes next. Read this book!

Lauri Rollings, CEO, Lauri Rollings and Associates, podcaster, *PERSONNELity*

Books that are short, easy to read and understand, packed with common sense and wisdom, full of meaningful stories, loaded with insightful quotes, and that offer practical, life-enhancing advice are hard to find. This is one of those rare books. Mark Matteson has given us a wonderful guide to a rewarding life that we'll want to revisit often.

Hal Urban, author, *Life's Greatest Lessons* and *The Power of Good News*

I just finished reading Mark Matteson's new book, As We THINK, So We BECOME. *His writing, told through stories, is very enjoyable to read but also pushes me to think about the message and how I live my life, in business and with family. I was particularly glad he revisited 'Just for Today.' It's a wonderful reminder of what we can accomplish by setting goals that are simply worked on one day at a time. When I finish one of Mark's books, I always have a smile on my face and a positive thought to work on.*

Chuck Lencheck, sr. vice president for channel development, Service Partners

I love Mark Matteson and I love this book! Success is the result of great habits. Mark's approach is simple and sound: Discipline your thoughts and take aligned action. What gives this book its genius is the way it is constructed. Mark lays out the exercises and gives us the direction and space—literally, right in the book!—to practice and develop success habits. Mark is thoughtful and vulnerable, but isn't afraid to "get real" and get to the root of our challenges. This is a must-read and must-do book!

Ellen Rohr, president, Zoom Drain Franchise

Are you willing to spend twenty-two minutes a day for twenty-one days to make an impactful and positive difference in your life? This is exactly what Mark Matteson has done in As We THINK So We BECOME *with his common-sense strategies.*

Tom Jackson, CEO, Jackson Systems & Supply

What a great book! We can accomplish anything we put our minds to—and my own books and radio shows have helped thousands of people accomplish exactly what this book says: "As we think so we become. This book checks all the boxes, reminding us that "Anything you put your mind to you can accomplish!"

Rick Solofsky, Medicare and group-insurance expert, author, ***Medicare Decoded*** **and** ***Health Insurance Revolution***

Once again, Mark Matteson delivers a wealth of knowledge broken into easily digestible chapters. From leadership and parenting to business management, this book has all the golden nuggets. Another life-changing and perception-altering read. Great job, Mark!

Shawn Mitchell, CEO and president, Modern Mechanical, and chair of the Loudoun County Chamber of Commerce

Mark's life shares, experiences, and stories inspire us all to take a good hard look at ourselves, and ask how and why we want to navigate life and business. The "Man in the Mirror" content in your new book enthusiastically challenged me to take action in my own life, one step at a time! Thank you for the privilege.

Bob Oates, president, Bob Oates Plumbing

Mark does an amazing job teaching through stories. His ability to relate to people allows him to open the mind of anyone willing to listen and inspire them to be their best self. His presence is a gift!

Dustin Flatten, president, Active Heating SD

AS WE THINK SO WE BECOME

MARK MATTESON

AS WE
THINK

SO WE
BECOME

— 22 WAYS —

to Change Your Thinking and
Live Your Best Life Right Now

Ugly Dog Publishing

ALSO BY MARK MATTESON

Freedom from Fear
Freedom from Fear Forever
A Simple Choice
It's About TIME
Freedom from FAT
Old Light Through New Windows

EBOOKS

Wag More, Bark Less
Sales Success Stories
Customer Service Excellence
Presenting Like a Pro
You Don't Have to Be Sick to Get Better
Sparking Sales Success (How to Enjoy a 75% Close Ratio)

Published by **Ugly Dog Publishing,** Edmonds, WA

ISBN 978-0-9995350-5-9

Designed and printed in the United States of America

Contents

Foreword by Andrew Bennett   1
Chapter 1 – The Strangest Secret   5
Chapter 2 – On Anger . . . A Choice   10
Chapter 3 – Shrink or Stretch?   17
Chapter 4 – Freedom from Fear   22
Chapter 5 – Action Cures Fear   30
Chapter 6 – Just for Today (Revisited)   36
Chapter 7 – The Guy in the Glass   41
Chapter 8 – The Bamboo   45
Chapter 9 – Sparks of Truth   50
Chapter 10 – Digital Dialogue Debrief   54
Chapter 11 – The Old Man   60
Chapter 12 – B.D.H. = Being, Doing, Having!   63
Chapter 13 – On Goals   68
Chapter 14 – Who Am I?   72
Chapter 15 – Who Might I Still Become?   77
Chapter 16 – "Um, ya know, and uh, like . . ."   106
Chapter 17 – A List of Lists   113
Chapter 18 – My Real Clients Are . . .   118
Chapter 19 – Anchors Away!   124
Chapter 20 – Pluck a Thistle and Plant a Rose   131
Chapter 21 – A.N.T.s at Your Picnic?   137
Chapter 22 – Goals? Thanks, Earl!   145
About Mark Matteson   151

Foreword

I lost many people in my childhood, and it set me on an accelerated path to figuring out the meaning of life and how to make the most of it. I'd never met anyone who came close to my own commitment to personal and professional development until I met Mark Matteson.

We met at EDGE Learning Institute in 1993, where we'd both gone to learn the business of training and development from Mark's mentor, the late, great Bob Moawad. A few years later, each of us felt called to start our own business. Mark wanted to serve people in sales and service, and I was drawn to helping grow leaders, and after all these years, I've still never met anyone so earnestly committed to helping others grow while relentlessly continuing his own development.

It seems like Mark's every waking hour is spent learning and practicing new approaches, new ways to become a better professional and a better person. He isn't just a pusher of theories and clever ideas, he's a practitioner, out in the field, learning new approaches, trying them out, adjusting and getting better, and then sharing what he learns with others to help them improve as well.

There's an overarching purpose to Mark's life: To become the best person he can be and to help others do the same. I wish you could spend a day with him. You'd undoubtedly enjoy some good coffee, and he'd make you feel like you were the only other person in the room. Mark would give you his undivided attention and ask you questions because he wants to know who you are. As he listens, he would do so with appreciation, stopping you occasionally to tell you what he admires about you. Mark loves people and he wants the best for everyone he meets. That's the bottom line.

Over the years, Mark and I have been there to support each other. It always comes down to how we play the "inner game"—how we manage our thoughts. In this book, Mark offers what he's learned over many years of hard experience. It comes down to this: The quality of your life depends on the quality of your thinking, and in *As We Think, So We Become,* Mark gives you everything you need to manage your most valuable asset—your mind.

The book you hold in your hands is invaluable. It's a powerful toolkit that will change your life.

Please help yourself to some of Mark's energy and commitment. Study this book. Practice some new techniques. You'll be more successful and fulfilled, and you'll positively impact everyone in your orbit.

Andrew Bennett, president
Bennett Performance Group

—One—

The Strangest Secret

A man is what he thinks about all day long.
Ralph Waldo Emerson

I **grew up poor.** Oh, I never missed a meal, I always had clothes on my back and a warm bed to sleep in, but my family was in the bottom level of the economic pyramid. When I was twelve years old, a girl in my seventh-grade class asked me a cutting question. "Why do you wear such weird clothes?" You see, I was in the "Have-Not" category. That was one of the very first rocks in my shoe. I didn't know it at the time, but I had begun a quest, a journey of discovery and awareness.

1989 was a magical year for me. I accepted a full-time sales position and committed myself to reading sales and personal-development books. I invested in audiocassette programs and played to them to the exclusion of everything else. As I listened, I kept hearing other speakers and authors reference something called *The Strangest Secret.* I got a copy and listened to it dozens of times.

Earl Nightingale was thirty-five in 1956 when he wrote and recorded *The Strangest Secret,* and he died in 1989, the same year I heard it. The original recording was made to be played on a Saturday morning to a small group of salespeople during Nightingale's absence. When he returned, he learned that the message had made such a positive impact that the salespeople wanted copies to share with their friends and family. Earl arranged with Columbia Records to duplicate the record to meet the many requests. Much to his surprise, in very little time without any real advertising or marketing, over a million copies had been sold. And he received a gold record. Earl called his message ***The Strangest Secret.***

Now, I invite you to sit back, relax, enjoy the original recording (Follow the link or scan the QR code).

https://youtu.be/F4s1Fyh4HAg

This excerpt might change your life:

Let me tell you something which, if you really understand it, will alter your life immediately. If you understand completely what I'm going to tell you from this moment on, your life will never be the same again . . . Doubt, fear, well, they will be things of the past. Here is the key to success and the key to failure. We become what we think about. Now let me say that again. **We become what we think about.**

A man's life is what his thoughts make of it.
Marcus Aurelius

Benjamin Disraeli said: "Everything comes if a man will only wait. I've brought myself by long meditation to the conviction that a human being with a settled purpose must accomplish it, and that nothing can resist a will that will stake even existence for its fulfillment."

A man is what he thinks about all day long.
Ralph Waldo Emerson

William James said, "The greatest discovery of my generation is that human beings can alter their lives by altering their attitudes of mind." And he also said, "We need only in cold blood act as if the thing in question were real, and it will become infallibly real by growing into such a connection with our life that it will become real. It will become so knit with habit and emotion that our interests in it will be those which characterize belief."

The Bible, in Mark 9:23, says, "If thou canst believe, all things are possible to him that believeth."

This little book is filled with ideas, information, strategies, and tools to assist you in improving your Magnificent Mind. I call it *Mental Management Magic!* Submitted for your approval . . .

I suggest you read a chapter a day and capture your "Ah-has" at the end of each chapter. We only need one good idea to change our lives for the better. If you only take ONE Action per chapter, you won't believe the changes you can make, like building a cathedral, one brick at a time.

Let's get started.

What One Action Will I Take?

_____

_____

_____

_____

_____

_____

_____

My Notes

_____

_____

_____

_____

_____

_____

_____

_____

_____

_____

_____

_____

_____

—Two—

On Anger . . . A Choice

One of the differences between assertiveness and aggressiveness is deciding which battles are worth fighting and which are not.
Thomas Harbin

Twenty years ago, I had a problem . . . with anger.

You say, "Hey, what guy doesn't get angry? What's the big deal?" Getting and staying angry is bad for your soul and will shorten your life. The short and long-term health issues that have been linked to unmanaged anger include headaches, digestive problems, abdominal pain, insomnia, increased anxiety, depression, high blood pressure, skin problems such as eczema, heart attack, and stroke. Other than that . . . well, you get the idea.

But what really got my attention and inspired me to seek a solution was the day my wife gave me an ultimatum: "Fix this, Mark. You are losing your family. Your boys are afraid of you." It was a wake-up call of the first order.

I called a mentor. He said, "My wife told me the same thing. Let's go to a seminar." He signed us up. I went with him. Then I went again on my own. The man conducting the session had a book list. I bought every one. I read ten books on the subject. Each was helpful in its own way, but I still struggled. Then I found the answers I sought in a 2018 book entitled, *Beyond Anger: A Guide for Men: How to Free Yourself from the Grip of Anger and Get More Out of Life* by Thomas J. Harbin, Ph.D., who freely admits that that HE had a problem with anger and decided to learn how to change. He says,

Rage is like a wounded animal. It attacks anything that moves. And as with a wounded animal, the attacks do nothing to ease the pain. Rage depersonalizes individual people and events into a faceless, nameless "them."

Rage is anger that never completely goes away. Unlike regular anger, it is not a response to a specific event; rather, it is a response set, or tendency. Rage sees personal attack in every disagreement. Rage causes you to feel threatened when there is no threat. And rage causes you to viciously counter-attack even a minor threat."

So it wasn't anger I needed to get on the other side of, it was *rage!* As hard as it was to admit to myself, there it was.

Thus began a difficult journey of self-discovery to get to the root cause of my irrational habit of lashing out at others. Here are the things I learned and practiced that changed me over time.

1. I read Harbin's book five times, twenty minutes a day. It was the only book I read for a month. I devoured it, studied it borrowed from it.
2. I kept an "Anger Journal" to write down my feelings and things that happened and how I responded to them, positive or negative.
3. I paid attention to my triggers. "What exactly sets me off?"

4. I began looking for "calm people" and observing their behavior.

5. I asked them, "How do you stay so cool and calm?" I wrote their answers in my journal.

6. I stopped watching *Seinfeld* and *Curb Your Enthusiasm*. Life truly does imitate art. There is nothing funny about rage.

7. I adopted the phrases "Oh well . . ." and "It is what it is . . ." and "No big deal . . ."

8. I stopped giving large amounts of time to negative, complaining, angry people. Anchors drag us down.

9. I began investing time hanging around positive, grateful, calm people. Speedboats pull us forward.

10. I prayed every time someone cut me off on the freeway, cut in line, said something rude, made me resentful. I used the "Serenity Prayer," but I called it "Praying for the Bastards!"

11. When I found myself getting angry, I would say "STOP!" aloud and take a few deep breaths.

12. I learned to ask the simple question, "How important is this, really?"

13. I wrote a goal on a 3 x 5 card: *"I am calm, cool and collected. Love and Tolerance are my code.*

> *I respond with grace and quiet dignity. Some-
> times I just walk away with a smile."*

14. I realized this was a marathon, not a fifty-yard
    dash. It was going to take a while.

15. I wrote about it, knowing one day I might be able
    to help someone else change, grow, and become.

16. I started helping others get on the other side of
    their anger and rage.

One of the differences between assertiveness and
aggression is deciding which battles are worth fighting
and which are not. Which takes more courage: rigidly
and inflexibly defending a principle, or demonstrating a
sense of perspective and a willingness to compromise
and walk away from a senseless argument?

In the final analysis, anger is a choice. I can *react*
with emotion and create more conflict, or I can *respond*
with grace and calm and find a civil solution that is win-
win.

I no longer have a rage issue. I still get angry at
times, but I know what to do when it happens. It's a temporary emotion. Feelings aren't facts. My family
WANTS to spend time with me. I am still married to

that woman twenty years after the fact. We are closer than ever. Why? Because I changed. So can you.

It takes work and a constancy of purpose. The juice is worth the squeeze . . .

To order Dr. Harbin's book, simply search for **Thomas Harbin** ***Beyond Anger*** at Amazon.com.

What One Action Will I Take?

_____

_____

_____

_____

_____

_____

_____

My Notes

_____

_____

_____

_____

_____

_____

_____

_____

_____

_____

_____

_____

—Three—

Shrink or Stretch?

People who have a sense of self-efficacy bounce back from failure; they approach things in terms of how to handle them rather than worrying about what can go wrong.
Albert Bandura

In 1997, I closed my first consulting engagement with a local TV station, The WB, Channel 22. I provided on-site sales training, team building, personal development, internal and external surveys, and monthly one-on-one coaching for the senior team. When the general manager introduced me to various members of his team and clients, he would say, "This is Mark Matteson, he is our in-house <u>shrink.</u>" Later, privately, I told him,

17

"You know, words trigger pictures and bring about emotion which leads to very specific behavior and the corresponding results. Why don't we say I'm the "in-house STRETCH! Because I am here to "stretch comfort zones." We scheduled a two-day "advance" (as opposed to a "retreat") and set very specific goals. We printed those goals onto posters and 3 x 5 cards for each office. After three delightful years of working together, the company achieved their goal of twenty million dollars a year (up from twelve million) and was purchased by the Tribune.

In these challenging times, are we *shrinking* or *stretching?*

In 1914, Thomas J. Watson, a former executive at the National Cash Register Company, became the general manager of C-T-R. According to company historians, "Watson implemented a series of effective business tactics. He preached a positive outlook, and his favorite slogan, 'THINK,' became a mantra for C-T-R's employees. Within eleven months of joining C-T-R, Watson became its president. The company focused on providing large-scale, custom-built tabulating solutions for businesses, leaving the market for small office products to others. During Watson's first four years, revenues more than doubled to nine million dollars. He also expanded the company's operations to Europe, South America, Asia and Australia." In 1924, the Computing-Tabulating-Recording Company was renamed the International Business Machines Corporation, or IBM.

He accomplished all this by advising his sales team to:

1. Double Their activity!
2. Invest time each day to THINK!
3. Maintain a positive, expectant mental mindset and a grateful attitude, with the focus on what they CAN do and forgetting what they CAN'T do!

Perhaps you're familiar with the *Yin and Yang* symbol.

Yin and yang (or yin-yang) is a complex relational concept that has developed over thousands of years. Briefly put, the meaning of yin and yang is that the universe is governed by a cosmic duality, a set of two opposing and complementing principles or cosmic energies that can be observed in nature.

In other words, danger or opportunity?

Risk or adventure?

Shrink or stretch?

It's a choice.

Which will you choose in this unprecedented time in world history?

What One Action Will I Take?

_____

_____

_____

_____

_____

_____

_____

My Notes

_____

_____

_____

_____

_____

_____

_____

_____

_____

_____

_____

_____

_____

—Four—

Freedom from Fear

F.E.A.R. is False Evidence Appearing Real!
Mark Matteson

What follows is an addendum to my first book, *Freedom from Fear.* It's sold over 200,000 copies worldwide and been translated into ten languages. To order your copy, go to

www.SparkingSuccess.net/store

What is fear? It's many things to many people. Ask ten people, "What is fear?" You'll get ten different answers. The number-one fear men have is public speaking; number two is death. That means most people would rather be in the casket than delivering the eulogy!

In my late twenties I read Napoleon Hill's *Think and Grow Rich,* a bestseller published in 1935 in the midst of the Great Depression. One chapter was called "How to Outwit the Six Ghosts of Fear." Here is *my* take on Mr. Hill's ghosts:

1. **The fear of poverty**. I grew up poor. I started working when I was twelve. I mowed lawns, washed windows, bought candy for a penny and sold it for a nickel. If I wanted something, I worked to pay for it. Poverty is a mindset. I have been out of money plenty of times, but being broke is a state of mind. Most millionaires have lost several fortunes before it finally stuck. It took billionaire Phil Knight over twenty years of hard work building Nike into a global force for him to finally become wealthy.

2. **The fear of criticism.** Put one crab in a bucket of water and he will climb right out. Drop five crabs in a bucket of water and none of them escape. Why? They pull each other down. What you think of me is none of my business! I have heard so many people say, "But what will THEY (people) say?" I have yet to find out who 'THEY' are! THEY can destroy your imagination, drive,

initiative, effort, and dreams. Walk away from THEY! Ignore THEY! To heck with THEY! Stay out of the bucket of crabs.

3. **The fear of ill health.** My mother used to say, "If you have your health, you have everything." How true. We don't miss our water until our well runs dry. It's not what happens to us but how we respond. Eat smart, work out, get plenty of sleep, drink lots of water, wash your hands like crazy, and have a positive expectation of the future. Oh yes, and be grateful.

4. **The fear of the loss of love.** I married up, and we have been together for over forty years. My friend Kevin said, "Man, that's a long sentence!" (He's been married for thirty-five years). If something were to happen to my wife, it would be hard. I would grieve, I suspect, for a long time. But life would go on. The Buddhists practice non-attachment. They learn to let things go. Everything in life has a beginning, a middle, and an end.

5. **The fear of old age.** "I met 'Dugout Doug', a former vaudevillian, when he was ninety-two. When I asked him how he was, he replied, "I'm so old, I don't even buy green bananas

anymore!" I remember thinking, *THAT is how I want to be when I grow up!* Many of the world's real achievements came from men and women who were well beyond the age of sixty-five. We live in a world that caters to the eighteen-to-forty-nine demographic. As long as a mind is clear and one takes care of their body (exercise four times a week—walking is still the best thing to do), there is no reason to stop contributing to humanity. Example: I am a more committed writer now than I was when I began twenty-four years ago at age thirty-eight.

6. **The fear of death.** One of my favorite quotes is, "I'm not afraid of dying, I just don't want to be there when it happens!" I have almost died three times: two surgeries and an automobile accident. I'm still here. I live one day at a time. I live every day as if it were my last because one day, I'll be right! I believe the best is yet to come . . .

If you find yourself full of fear, try the following Five Strategies:

1. **F.E.A.R.** is an acronym for **F**alse **E**vidence **A**ppearing **R**eal. It's a feeling and feelings are not facts. Moreover, these feelings are temporary.

2. Did you know that one square mile of fog is only twelve ounces of water? When we are driving our car and we come across a fog bank, most people slow down, some even stop. It's only water. It's temporary. Fog is like fear, it comes in many forms: doubt, worry, indecision, anger, judgment, prejudice and hate. Slow down, take a breath, and ask, "What am I afraid of?" and then write it down.

3. Ask yourself, "What is the worst thing that could happen if what I am worried about comes true?" Write it down. Then ask, "IF, then . . ." If then, could I live with that? Would I survive? Could I keep going? I will the bet you the farm you could. I have kept going. So can you.

4. Make a list of all the things you worry about. Write them all down. Then come back tomorrow and see how you feel. Colin Powell would do this when he was a five-star general. He said, "Things always look different in the morning."

5. The opposite of **FEAR** is **FAITH**. **F.A.I.T.H.** is also an acronym: Forgiving, Accepting,

Intentional, Thankful, **Humble**! Have faith. Pray and meditate. If prayer is talking to God, meditation is listening.

Babe Ruth said, "Never let the striking out get in your way." He ought to know. He holds the record for the most strikeouts, 1,330! He also hit 714 home runs. One day, in a double header, the Babe went 0-8, striking out eight times! A reporter asked him if he was worried. "Worried? Nah . . . I used to be a pitcher. I understand both sides of the plate. It's not me that should be worrying! I hit a home run in one out of every eleven at-bats! I wouldn't want to be pitching against me tomorrow . . . I'm DUE!" He hit two home runs the next day and the Yankees clinched the pennant (again)!

The most painful and debilitating fear is the unknown. Get the facts from the right sources.

Marianne Williamson wrote, *"Our deepest fear is not that we are inadequate. Our deepest fear is that we are powerful beyond measure. It is our light, not our darkness that most frightens us. We ask ourselves, 'Who am I to be brilliant, gorgeous, talented, fabulous?' Actually, who are you not to be? You are a child of God; You playing small does not serve the world . . . as we let our own light shine, we unconsciously give other people permission to do the same."*

Having said this, I would still rather deliver the eulogy than be in the casket. I don't get to choose when I die, but I can choose how I'll live. I'm going to live my life on purpose, giving it everything I have today, one day at a time, until . . .

What One Action Will I Take?

_____

_____

_____

_____

_____

_____

_____

My Notes

_____

_____

_____

_____

_____

_____

_____

_____

_____

_____

_____

_____

_____

—Five—

Action Cures Fear

Fear seems like a hundred-foot wall we cannot scale,
but it turns out it is paper thin and, with some courage
and effort, we can burst right through it!

The Great Depression was a severe worldwide economic depression that took place mostly during the 1930s, before most of us were born, beginning in the United States. The timing of the Great Depression varied across nations; in most countries, it started in 1929 and lasted until the late 1930s. It was the longest, deepest, and most widespread depression of the twentieth century. The Great Depression is commonly used as an example of how intensely the world's economy can decline. If history has taught us anything, it's that there have always been challenging times and, as a country, we came through them with longer legs for bigger strides!

Okay, so you're stuck working from home. You feel isolated, sad, lonely, afraid, and uncertain. Now what? How can you positively leverage your time working at home? Here is a list of things you CAN do to make the most of this unprecedented moment in time.

1. It's not a "Retreat." It's an "Advance." Words matter. They trigger pictures and bring about emotion. Change the language you use.

2. Continue to keep a safe distance from others. Six feet is what the CDC suggests. Wash your hands for twenty seconds ten times a day.

3. Invest in creative acts that add value to your organization. As we discussed in a previous chapter, Thomas J. Watson advised in the midst of the Depression, "THINK!" How can you add value to your organization? What new products or services can your company offer? (e.g., Become a Harbinger of Hope OR create a helpline, online coaching, etc.).

4. Focus your time and effort into your passions and hobbies.

5. Read those books you have always wanted to read, but never had the time to before. Why not go to my website, www.SparkingSuccess.net/store, and order some of mine?

6. Watch a TED Talk or an inspiring YouTube video daily.

7. Cook the things you love and share them with others.

8. Take daily walks with family or someone else you care about.

9. Start writing that book you have always promised yourself you would write. Send me an email and I will forward a special report entitled, "So You Want to Be a Writer?"

10. Listen to Podcasts. Mine can be found on my website or by clicking on the links at the end of this book.

11. Update your website with new content.

12. Virtually connect with your clients and discuss new insights to help them with their businesses.

13. Crowd source with others, leveraging their knowledge, talent, and wisdom to create something bigger than yourself.

14. Join an online community that fits with your interests and consider creating your own.

15. Organize your office space, purge your closets, clean it up.

16. Get lots of rest, drink lots of water, eat clean and healthy, and get plenty of sleep.

17. Learn to play an instrument. Take that old guitar out of the garage, dust it off, and play "Louie Louie."

18. Find ways to inject positive humor into your daily life.

19. Connect with old friends via Zoom, Skype or FaceTime. Renew vital long-term relationships with people you haven't seen in years.

20. Conclude your day by reviewing your goals (or set some new ones).

21. End each day with five things you are grateful for. Maintain a measure of optimism, enthusiasm, and helpfulness. We need each other.

22. Listen to Diana Krall sing "Pick Yourself Up" https://youtu.be/_p_JxDGVqXg Pay attention to the message in the lyrics. Great advice.

23. Remember what Einstein said: *"In the midst of every difficulty lies opportunity."*

24. If we keep doing what we have always done, we will keep getting what we have always got.
25. I need to remind myself, *"Everything has a beginning, a middle, and an end."*

One day, we will wake up and realize this was simply a very strange and scary time, and that we all lived through it. Ask any ninety year old what the Great Depression was like. Then sit back and listen. They lived to tell about it.

We will too.

PS: I offer long-distance coaching programs tailored to your needs and budgets. Call me today for a consultation, the first one is free . . . however, I only have a few spots left open, first come, first served. Call 206-697-0454, or email me at:

Mark.EnjoyTheJourney.Matteson@Gmail.com

What One Action Will I Take?

_____

_____

_____

_____

_____

_____

_____

My Notes

_____

_____

_____

_____

_____

_____

_____

_____

_____

_____

_____

_____

_____

—Six—

Just for Today (Revisited)

It takes 21-35 days to form a new, positive habit.
Mark Matteson

When I was twenty-four I discovered a book at a garage sale for fifty cents that changed my life, *How to Win Friends and Influence People,* by Dale Carnegie. It's a classic. I kept a copy of it in my service truck while working as a technician in 1982 and faithfully read a chapter a day. I recently plucked another Dale Carnegie gem from my bookshelf, *How to Stop Worrying and Start Living.* Filled with great stories and fascinating guidance. It might be even better than the first one is. In the chapter "Seven Ways to Peace and Happiness" I rediscovered one of my favorite bits of advice, written by Sybil F. Partridge in 1908. Carnegie writes, "I found this program so inspiring, I gave away hundreds of copies."

Now it's my turn. Here you go, some hundred-year-old advice, (paraphrased for clarification and to my own personal application):

1. *Just for today, I will be happy. This assumes what Abraham Lincoln said is true, that "Most folks are about as happy as they make their minds up to be." Happiness is from within; it is not a matter of externals.*
2. *Just for today, I will adjust myself to what is, and not try to adjust everything to my own desires. I will take my family, my business and my luck as they come and fit myself to them. (In a word, Acceptance!)*
3. *Just for today, I will take care of my body. I will exercise it, care for it, nourish it, not abuse or neglect it, so that it will be a perfect machine for my bidding. (I will work out daily and eat clean and smart.)*
4. *Just for today, I will strengthen my mind, I will learn something useful. I will not be a mental*

loafer. I will read a book that requires effort, thought, and concentration. (I will write something that serves others.)

5. Just for today, I will exercise my soul in three ways: I will do somebody a good turn and not get found out. I will do at least two things today I don't want to do, as William James says, just for the exercise and discipline.

6. Just for today, I will be agreeable. I will look as well as I can, dress as becomingly as possible, talk low, act courteously, be liberal with praise, criticize not at all, nor find fault with anything or anyone; and not try to regulate, not improve anyone (but myself).

7. Just for today, I will live through this day only, not to tackle my whole life problem at once. I can do things for twelve hours that would appall me if I had to keep them up for a lifetime.

8. Just for today, I will have a program. I will write down what I expect to do every hour. I may not follow it exactly, but I will have it. It will eliminate two pests: hurry and indecision.

9. Just for today, I will have a quiet half-hour all by myself and relax. In this half-hour sometimes I will think of God, so as to get a little more

perspective into my life. (I will give thanks for my blessings.)

10. *Just for today, I will be unafraid, especially I will not be afraid to be happy, to enjoy what is beautiful, to love, to believe those I love, love me. Just for today.*

I wonder what would happen if I printed this, pasted it on my bathroom mirror, and read it aloud for thirty days as a test . . . nah! I don't want to be *too* healthy . . .

What One Action Will I Take?

_____

_____

_____

_____

_____

_____

_____

My Notes

_____

_____

_____

_____

_____

_____

_____

_____

_____

_____

_____

_____

—Seven—

The Guy in the Glass

To thine own self be true.
William Shakespeare

Some people go to church for show, to impress other people; others go to church to worship. Some people donate to charity to look good to others, others donate because it's a good cause they believe in and often do it anonymously. What is your Spirit of Intent?

Years ago, I met a man who began every meeting with a poem. When I asked him who wrote it, he didn't know. With a quick internet search I discovered it was Peter Dale Wimbrow, usually known as Dale Wimbrow (June 6, 1895 – January 26, 1954). He was an American composer, radio artist, and writer.

He is best known for the poem ***The Guy in the Glass,*** written in 1934.

When you get what you want in your struggle for wealth
And the world makes you King for a Day,
Just go to the mirror and look at yourself
And see what that man has to say.

For it isn't your father, or mother or wife
Whose judgment on you must pass,
The fellow whose verdict counts most in your life
It's the one staring back from the glass.

Some people may think you are a straight shooting chum
And call you a wonderful guy,
But the man in the glass says you're only a bum,
If you can't look him straight in the eye.

He's the fellow to please, never mind all the rest,
For he's with you clear up to the end,
And you have passed your most difficult test
If the man in the glass is your friend.

You may fool the whole world down the pathway of life
And get pats on the back as you pass,
But your final reward will be heartaches and tears
If you have cheated the man in the glass.

Shakespeare said the same thing in fewer words:

To thine own self be true.

What One Action Will I Take?

_____

_____

_____

_____

_____

_____

_____

_____

My Notes

_____

_____

_____

_____

_____

_____

_____

_____

_____

_____

_____

_____

_____

—Eight—

The Bamboo

Anger is an acid that can do more harm to the vessel in which it is stored than to anything on which it is poured.
Mark Twain

I was six years old in 1963 and we lived in Yokohama, Japan. Yosh-ko-san was my nanny and she took me everywhere she went. We would often stop at the same temple before going home. One day, an elderly gentleman was digging a hole. Like Curious George, I asked her why. Yosh-ko-san asked him in Japanese, on my behalf, what he was doing (she already knew). He explained he was planting a bamboo shoot.

"The process is simple," she explained with love. "Take an eighteen-inch shoot, dig a hole three feet deep, and cover with soil." Smiling, she put her arm around me and said, "The most important part takes the longest. He must come back every day for a year and water the shoot. Nothing will happen. He must come back for another year, every day, and water. Nothing will happen. He must come back a third year, every day, and water. Nothing will happen. He must come back a fourth year, every day, and water. Nothing will happen. He must come back for a fifth year, every day, and water. Nothing will happen . . . until the beginning of the sixth year. Because he was faithful and watered the bamboo shoot for 1,825 days, something magical happens. The little shoot, at the beginning of the sixth year, will grow NINETY FEET IN SIX WEEKS!!!

Yes, that's right. It will grow almost three feet a day for a month and a half!

My skill development, my business, my spiritual life, my fitness level is just like that Bamboo. When the growth happens, abundance happens seemingly overnight, but it takes about seven or eight years of hard work or ten thousand hours, whichever comes first.

Paying the price in advance and staying the course no matter what is the secret of success.

My spiritual life and corresponding development is like that bamboo. It has taken longer to master than any other aspect of my life-quest.

One of my spiritual mentors taught me . . .

I must arise from the death of selfishness and put on a new life of integrity. All my old defects and temptations must be laid in the grave . . . and a new existence rise from the ashes. Yesterday is gone. My old life is just that, old. I forgive myself. I am becoming a new person. IF I am honestly trying to do God's will today, I have no regrets. Today is here, the time of resurrection and renewal. I must start now, today, to build a new life of complete faith and trust in God, and a determination to do his will.

He went on to say, *"Expectations are pre-meditated resentments. Resentment? It's like taking poison and hoping the other person will die."*

On page 552 of the third edition of the classic book *Alcoholics Anonymous*, written by Bill Wilson, a woman tells her story:

An article I read in a magazine said: 'If you have a resentment you want to be free of, if you will pray for that person or thing that you resent, you will be free. If you will ask in prayer for everything you want for yourself to be given to them, you will be free. Ask for their health, their prosperity, their happiness, and you will be free . . . Do it every day for two weeks and you will find you have come to mean it and to want it for them, and you will realize that where you used to feel bitterness and resentment and hatred, you now feel compassionate understanding and love.

What I have been learning is *FORGIVENESS* is one of the antidotes for *RESENTMENT.* When I FORGIVE someone it's not them that is healed, it's me! I need to surrender my RESENTMENTS daily! Life is too short to BE-LITTLE, hold grudges, and hang on to negative emotions.

I wish Yosh-ko-san were still alive. I would take her to a temple and pray with her, give her a big hug, and tell her, "Thank you . . . I love you so much."

She was my first great teacher. I have some watering to do!

What One Action Will I Take?

_____

_____

_____

_____

_____

_____

_____

My Notes

_____

_____

_____

_____

_____

_____

_____

_____

_____

_____

_____

_____

_____

—Nine—

Sparks of Truth

He can who <u>thinks</u> he can.
Henry Ford

Emmett Fox was a pastor, an author, a 1930s New York City newspaper columnist, and a major influence on Bill Wilson, the co-founder of AA. What follows are some of his best quotes from an old, rare book I just happened to find in a used book store over twenty years ago entitled *Sparks of Truth.*

❑ *Mind is cause, and experience is effect.*
❑ *Take it easy.*
❑ *A healthy body grows out of a happy mind.*

50

❏ *If you have no time for prayer and meditation, you will have lots of time for sickness and trouble.*

❏ *Act as though it was and it will be.*

❏ *If you are living the spiritual life, you are entitled to peace of mind and harmonious progress. Should these things be lacking, it is your duty to set aside a reasonable time each day for prayer and spiritual reading.*

❏ *GOD is ready the moment you are.*

❏ *Peace of mind first and all things will follow that.*

❏ *You can have anything in life that you really want, but you must be prepared to take the responsibilities that go with it.*

❏ *Let go and let God.*

❏ *Criticism of others is the hallmark of failure.*

❏ *Face the facts candidly, then you can change them.*

❏ *Your destiny depends entirely upon your own mental conduct. Never forget that the circumstances of your life tomorrow are molded by your mental conduct of today.*

❏ *Be still and know that I am God.*

❏ *Make up your mind. Do one thing or the other. Stick to your choice.*

❏ *Don't be a slave to other people's opinion. Do what you know is right.*

51

❏ *Compare and compete with your own best self.*

❏ *Never tell people about the fine thing you are about to do. Wait until you have done it. Talking about your plans before they have actually materialized is the surest way to destroy them.*

❏ *Clean up your own house and never look back.*

❏ *Under any circumstances you must keep your own thought poised, tolerant, and kindly. Remember the Golden Rule.*

❏ *Radiate happiness and you help and inspire everyone you meet. Cultivate happiness and then you must radiate it, for it cannot be concealed. Misery can be hidden, but happiness can no more be kept a secret than garlic.*

❏ *Trying to pray is praying.*

❏ *Peace of mind is the one thing that matters. There is absolutely nothing else in the world which is equal in value to it. Nothing else that life can offer is more important than that and yet it seems to be about the last thing that many people work for.*

It would have been something to spend time with Mr. Fox. Thank God we have his books. He lives on in his writing and the legacy he left behind.

What One Action Will I Take?

_____

_____

_____

_____

_____

_____

_____

My Notes

_____

_____

_____

_____

_____

_____

_____

_____

_____

_____

_____

_____

_____

—Ten—

Digital Dialogue Debrief

Have you seen the 2003 movie *Lost in Translation*? Bill Murray plays an over-the-hill movie star who is hired to promote a Japanese Whiskey in Tokyo. He is being paid a princely sum to hock a product he doesn't necessarily believe in or use. They spoil him rotten, putting him up in a five-star hotel, but he has lost his mojo. It's a bittersweet tale of unrequited love and humor in a clash of cultures.

By definition, the title means *the inability to understand due to having been poorly translated*, as in, "I tried reading the instruction manual but many of the steps were unfortunately **lost in translation**."

In the digital age in which we live and work, many things are lost in translation. Why is that? It's simple really. 55% of all communication is non-verbal, 38%

extra-verbal, and 7% are the words. When we speak to each other in person, all those elements are in play, but in an email or text the non-verbal elements are conspicuously missing. We can only do so much with UPPER CASE LETTERS and emojis like :-) or :-(

What to do? Zoom is helping (assuming you show your face and are fully dressed!), but as more and more people work from home, when something is gained, something is lost—in translation.

What follows is a *Digital Dialogue Debrief,* some simple ideas to improve our efforts to communicate effectively with friends, colleagues, family, and vendors.

1. **Speak in the First Person.** Don't say YOU or WE when you mean I. When I use YOU, I am, in effect, "Should-ing" on you—moreover, I am not taking personal responsibility for my actions and decisions. When I use WE it's misleading and manipulative if not based on an actual survey or consensus.

2. **Ask Questions (Instead of Giving Orders).** It took me fifteen years of marriage to learn this one. My wife has used this to great effect: "You feel like going out tonight?" I used to say, "Um, okay, yeah, sure . . ." Now it's MY idea. These days,

because I am hip and aware, I say, "It sounds like you do . . ." Education is a beautiful thing.

3. **Use Tact and Diplomacy.** Ben Franklin was a master at this. He would listen to another person's position and then say, "I could be wrong, I often am . . ." and then state his position. He would follow up with, "Have you ever considered . . ." or "What if we . . ." or "Let's look at both sides, then we can make an informed decision . . ."

4. **Use Self-Effacing Humor.** After a Keynote, a client once told me, "I love your self-defecating humor!" I knew what he meant. (Insert emoji crying with laughter here! :-) When I poke fun at myself, you don't get to. Furthermore, I am telling you that I am comfortable in my own skin and am willing to take interpersonal risks to build rapport and friendships.

5. **Be Quick to Admit Mistakes.** Personal responsibility has taken a beating. It's healing to hear someone, especially someone in a position of leadership, say, "I dropped the ball—I sliced in the woods, please forgive me. I don't know what I was thinking. That was thoughtless. In future, I will be more mindful." By the way, there is a difference between an apology and an amend. An apology is

"I'm sorry . . ." without a change in future behavior. They are two very different things.

6. **Give a Person a Fine Reputation to Live Up To**. Dale Carnegie tells the story of "Tommy," the troubled kid a teacher inherited. Rather than believing what other teachers said of Tommy, the first day of school she looks him straight in the eye and says, "Tommy, I understand you are a natural leader—I'm going to depend on you to make this class the best class in the school." She reinforced her statement over the next few days by complimenting his progress to prove her prediction.

7. **Praise Progress.** Be hearty in your approbation and lavish in your praise whenever you see any kind of positive change in the behavior of others. "See, I told you—great job on that report. I'm so proud of your progress. One day, you'll have my job!" Praise pays.

One thing is certain: If I practice these principles with people I care about, my communication skills online (and in person) will be more effective. I also need to remember that nothing beats a face-to-face meeting. I guess I'll settle for Zoom for now. At least you get to see my facial expressions and hand gestures. After all, that's 55% of the message.

Last week, a guy cut me off on the freeway and gave me half a peace sign!? I got the message without exchanging a word. His message wasn't lost in translation!

I need to watch that movie with Bill Murray again— I think it's on Netflix.

What One Action Will I Take?

My Notes

—Eleven—

The Old Man

"What kind of people live in your town?"

An old man sat on the edge of town in a rocking chair, whittling with his knife. A stranger with a frown and a furrowed brow approached him and asked, "Say, old man, what kind of people live in this town?"

Looking up from his work, and pausing for effect, the old man inquired, "What kind of people lived in the town you left?"

"Oh, they were mean, critical, negative, and angry. I couldn't wait to leave!"

"That is exactly the kind of people you will find in this town. You might not be very happy here. I hear the

*next town is a little better." The grumpy stranger moved
on without a word of thanks.*

*About an hour later another man, wearing a big
smile, walked up to the old man. "Good afternoon, sir.
Pardon me, but could you tell me what kind of people
live in this town?"*

*Smiling back at the young man, the old man in-
quired, "What kind of people were in the last town you
lived in?"*

*"Oh, they were amazing, kind, generous, thoughtful,
I hated to leave."*

*"You'll find the same kind of people in this town.
Welcome! I hope you stay a long time."*

My wife heard me tell that story a few times to our
children as they were growing up. Whenever she hears
me grumbling, complaining, or taking a turn to "Negative Town," she smiles and says: *"What kind of people
live in your town?"*

I still have to work at it. I probably should buy a
rocking chair and invest in a good sharp knife. I've got
some whittling to do!

What One Action Will I Take?

_____

_____

_____

_____

_____

_____

_____

_____

My Notes

_____

_____

_____

_____

_____

_____

_____

_____

_____

_____

_____

_____

_____

_____

—Twelve—

B.D.H.=Being, Doing, Having!

Success comes from knowing that you did your best to become the best that you are capable of becoming.
John Wooden

Did you know that most lottery winners end up broke, divorced, and miserable within five years? Why is that? It's because it was simply luck. They didn't earn what they were given. If someone hands you a million dollars, you better *become* a millionaire fast.

A life of abundance, joy, and peace of mind is what most people want, but 96% of the population goes about it all wrong. They have the *process* backwards. They say, "I want to HAVE more things or more money in order to DO more of what I want so I will BE more happy." The way it actually works for the top 4% is the reverse. You must first BE who you really are or wish to be, and work for years to BECOME that person; then you are driven to DO the things to earn the money, joy, abundance, and peace of mind. Only then will you HAVE what you really want. Moreover, you will keep what you justly earned.

Think of this process as a triangle. The points are not in conflict with each other. They all exist simultaneously. They are earned. Each side supports the other. However, it must begin with BEING first, then the DOING to earn the HAVING!

BEING

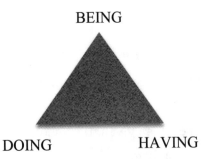

DOING   HAVING

We need to connect with our BEING, to help us focus and facilitate the DOING, to deepen, expand, and align our HAVING.

*For me, becoming isn't about arriving some-
where or achieving a certain aim. I see it instead
as forward motion, a means of evolving, a way to
reach continuously toward a better self. The
journey doesn't end.*

Michelle Obama

If you want to BECOME the very best version of
yourself, let's say the Top Sales-Person in your company, focus first on these short-term BECOMING
Goals:

1. BECOME a world-class active listener.
2. BECOME an activity madman or madwoman.
3. BECOME someone who learns how to sell
   value, not price.
4. BECOME a person who offers a choice of yeses.
5. BECOME professionally persistent, keeping strict
   accounts and staying in touch with prospects.
6. BECOME someone who goes the extra mile for
   clients.
7. BECOME someone who reads sales books daily.
8. BECOME someone who attends every seminar.

9. BECOME someone who keeps a journal and asks, "What did I do well?" and "What are my growth opportunities for the next call?"
10. BECOME someone who knows how to overcome objections with compassion, kindness, and tact.

You may never win the lottery, but you CAN focus on BECOMING the person who has learned this simple lesson: BE first, DO second, HAVE third! You'll be glad you did!

What One Action Will I Take?

_____

_____

_____

_____

_____

_____

_____

_____

My Notes

_____

_____

_____

_____

_____

_____

_____

_____

_____

_____

_____

_____

_____

—Thirteen—

On Goals

*The greatest reason for setting and achieving goals is
who we must become in order to achieve them!*
Jim Rohn

I **wrote the following poem** after my first grand-child, Penelope Jean Matteson, was born, to be read
to her on her twelfth birthday. Submitted for your ap-proval . . .

On Goals
*First I work on goals,
Then they work on me,
It's a kind of mental magic;
To manifest what IS to be.*

The first time feels a bit funny,
It's a stretch of my comfort zone,
Yet the next thing I know, achievement!
All because I decided, asked, and studied alone.

The mind is capable of so much more
Than I ever think I can;
Ask, seek, knock on that closed door,
And abracadabra, I'm a goal-achieving fan.

I was told that decision, desire, and a dedicated mind
Bring about a shift in my mental state;
If I stay on this path, I'll find
What I want wants me, soon or late.

The first time I set a meaningful goal
I was asked to affirm it aloud;
The very thing that whispers to my soul
Would soon be the thing that makes me proud.

So I gave it a try, saying them five times a day,
And wouldn't you know it, I formed a new belief;
I began the process April 1 and achieved it mid-May.
Enthusiasm and gratitude replaced my doubt and grief.

Why not YOU, my mentor said,
With the sincerity and authority of a pastor.
And wouldn't you know it, I achieved it,
Changing from student to master.

If it's to be, it's up to me,
I've heard it said before,
Transformed from skeptic to true believer,
I'll be setting goals, evermore.

What One Action Will I Take?

My Notes

—Fourteen—

Who Am I?

The two most important days of your life? The day you
were born and the day you find out why.
Mark Twain

Who am I? How did I become the person I am?
What influenced my values, beliefs, habits, and
attitudes? Who were the biggest influences from my
childhood? If our life is a novel, examining each chapter
of our childhood is vital to understanding the person we
become.

Re-reading Bruce Springsteen's extraordinary 2016
memoir *Born to Run* (which took him seven years to
write) gives us a glimpse of the answer. On page 414,

writing with a kind of brutal honesty few authors do, he posits:

> *Those whose love we wanted but could not get, we emulate. It is dangerous but makes us feel closer, gives us an illusion of the intimacy we never had. It stakes our claim upon that which was rightfully ours but denied. I'm a repairman. That is part of my job. So I, who'd never done a week's worth of manual labor in my life (hail, hail rock and roll!), put on a factory worker's clothes, my father's clothes, and went to work.*

When I consider the professional path I chose over twenty-five years ago, to become a professional speaker and author, I reflect back upon my parents' natural and lifelong affinities. It was only then that my own path became crystal clear. I am my father's son. He was a tremendous athlete, all-state in three sports. He went on to coach every sport when, as athletic director of an air force base in Yokohama, Japan, he inspired, encouraged, and taught men the value of hard work, commitment to the team, and the value of selfless dedication to winning. My career as a coach, consultant, teacher, and speaker had its roots in my father's love of sports.

We watched sports together on TV hundreds of times. When I committed to basketball at thirteen, it was my dad who built the court in the backyard. We played H-O-R-S-E and one-on-one until our respective competitive juices clashed like the titans of old. With my father, everything was a competition, even cribbage!

My mother had a passion for the arts. She loved writing letters and journaling, music, plays, theater, films, especially musicals. Psychologists claim the person you are by age five is who you'll be the rest of your life. What I consistently heard coming through the stereo speakers at that impressionable age were show tunes: *West Side Story, The King and I, Oklahoma.* My mother was an extra in a few films, including Woody Allen's *What's Up, Tiger Lily?* (A low-rent Japanese spy flick with dubbed dialogue). Later in life she acted in community theater. She was also a voracious reader of books and magazines and kept a journal her whole life. Her secret ambition was to write a book. Her memoir was self-published just before she died.

When I consider these influences—the writing, coaching, speaking and, yes, acting, it's easy to see how I gravitated to speaking, coaching, consulting and, yes, becoming an author.

When I step on a stage to teach, coach, inspire, and entertain, I am channeling my parents. Bruce Springsteen was right. I put on my father's clothes and went to work.

Who are you? Mark Twain helped me understand WHY I was born. I know who I am. Do you?

What One Action Will I Take?

_____

_____

_____

_____

_____

_____

_____

_____

My Notes

_____

_____

_____

_____

_____

_____

_____

_____

_____

_____

_____

_____

_____

—Fifteen—

Who Might I Still Become?

Once you agree upon the price you and your family
must pay for success, it enables you to ignore the mi-
nor hurts, the opponent's pressure,
and the temporary failures.
Vince Lombardi

Ray Kroc, the founder of the McDonald's Corporation, wrote a 1977 memoir entitled *Grinding It Out.* (Michael Keaton played him brilliantly in the 2016 movie *The Founder*). The one big takeaway for me was the quote, *"You are either green and growing OR ripe and rotting!"* So true. I am either consciously getting better or unconsciously getting worse. There is no neutral in life or business.

Over the last few months I have been giving serious thought to what I believe, and gaining clarity on my values, my philosophy. Becoming a grandfather has inspired me to consider my legacy, that is, what I would like to leave behind for future generations. Will I be a ghost or an ancestor? How do I want to be remembered? What has evolved are *Six Operating Beliefs,* or ways of being, that I aspire to. It's really who I want to be when no one is looking. Let's call it *Who Might I Still Become? (Twelve Words to Live By).*

Work Smart
Be Kind
Have Fun
Keep Learning
Help Others
Give Thanks

Work Smart

*People who work hard and people who work smart
have different measures of success.*
Jacob Morgan

A lot of very successful people I know believe in hard work. It's one of the reasons they are successful. My father believed it, yet despite working hard, he never made any real money. I have learned a few simple things over the years that have helped me earn a fine living, enjoy balance, peace of mind, and effectiveness. I coached my boys in basketball, sixty games a year for over ten years. It was a lot of work. I do not regret an hour or a dollar I invested in those hectic, challenging, and glorious years. I wouldn't trade that time for all the tea in China.

What follows are tips for *Working Smarter*:

1. What is the best and highest use of my time? I need to soar with my strengths and delegate my weaknesses.
2. Do first things first, one thing at a time, and finish what I start.

3. The 80-20 Rule: Pareto's Principle posits that 80% of the results come from 20% of the effort. Focus my time, energy, and effort on the 20%! I Plan my work and work my plan every day.

4. Check my email only two or three times a day. Breakfast, lunch, and dinner are excellent times.

5. Limit time on social media. An hour a day is plenty.

6. Be mindful of WHO you invest time with and WHAT you allow into your head. You will be the same person in five years but for two things, the BOOKS you read and the PEOPLE with whom you associate. Associate with SPEED-BOATS and stay away from ANCHORS!

7. Know when to walk away. Some projects, some people, some situations drain your time and energy. It's okay to say NO, smile, and walk away!

How can you work smarter today and not harder today? What do you need to STOP doing that is holding you back from becoming the best version of you? What do you need to START doing?

What One Action Will I Take?

_____

_____

_____

_____

_____

_____

_____

_____

My Notes

_____

_____

_____

_____

_____

_____

_____

_____

_____

_____

_____

_____

_____

_____

_____

Be Kind

Human freedom involves our capacity to respond (not react), to choose one response toward which we wish to throw our weight.
Rollo May

There is a difference between being nice and being kind. My mother was British. She was almost always polite and nice. Yet, as it is with all of us, she wasn't always kind. They are not the same thing. Being nice is an act, a mask we wear. Being kind is a way of living, a philosophy. Being kind sounds simple and it is; it's just not easy. I've always admired kind people. I want to be more like them. It seems to me they travel through their days with a kind of grace. The dictionary defines grace as *undeserved favor*. Grace leaves pleasure and calm in its wake. Becoming kind is a marathon, not a fifty-yard dash. The late great Mr. Fred Rogers believed in what he called *Radical Kindness!* I like that. Today I am working on being kind versus being nice.

According to David R. Hamilton, PhD, there are five side-benefits to kindness that improve our health, peace of mind, and joy:

1. **Kindness makes us happier.** It releases and elevates the levels of dopamine in the brain. It provides a natural high, similar to how we feel after a good workout or belly laugh.

2. **Kindness is good for our heart.** It generates an emotional warmth and produces oxytocin in the brain and body. This, in turn, releases nitric oxide in the blood vessels, causing them to dilate and lower our blood pressure, which acts as a cardio-protective agent, thus reducing the risk of heart disease.

3. **Kindness slows aging.** The reduction of free radicals and inflammation slows aging in the human body. Dr. Hamilton notes that compassion has similarly been linked to activity in the vagus nerve, which also regulates heart rate and controls inflammation.

4. **Kindness improves relationships.** Connecting with one another is actually a genetic predisposition. Hamilton contends, "Our evolutional ancestors had to learn to cooperate with one another.

The stronger the emotional bonds within groups, the greater the chances of survival. Kindness genes are etched into the human genome." As a result, kindness builds new relationships and boosts existing ones.

5. **Kindness is contagious.** Just as colds and viruses are contagious in a bad way, so is kindness in a good way. "When we are kind, we inspire others to be kind and it actually creates a ripple effect that spreads outwards to our friends and family."

What actions will you take today to demonstrate kindness towards others?

What One Action Will I Take?

_____

_____

_____

_____

_____

_____

_____

_____

My Notes

_____

_____

_____

_____

_____

_____

_____

_____

_____

_____

_____

_____

_____

Have Fun

Searching is half the fun:
Life is much more manageable when thought of as a
scavenger hunt as opposed to a surprise party.
Jimmy Buffett

I love to play, watch, coach, and read about basketball. It was my very first magnificent obsession.

I was bit by the basketball bug at age thirteen. I've had over fifty years of fun. I can't get enough. Junior high, high school, college, professional, it doesn't matter.

I love movies. I lived in Japan from 1959 to 1963. My mother would send us off to the base theater on Saturday with twenty-five cents: fifteen cents to get in, five cents for popcorn, and five cents for a soda. I was in heaven. The family joke was that when my older brother took me to see *Ben-Hur* when I was five years old, I fell asleep during the famous chariot race scene but was awake for all the love scenes. I watch a movie every day. It's still fun.

86

I love books. I read at least two a week: non-fiction, biographies, history, self-help, spiritual, wellness, business, fiction, it doesn't matter. I carry one with me everywhere I go. I have dozens loaded up on my phone. I listen to them on long drives, a habit I've kept since 1989. I call it Windshield University.

I believe we need to build fun into our day. My father used to say, "Work hard, play hard." I say, "Work Smart, Play Smart." Surrender to the fun. Toss a ball with your dog. Get on the floor with your grandchildren. Read a book to a child. Make the time to watch a sunset. Carpe diem.

When was the last time you really had fun? What positive activities bring you the most joy?

What One Action Will I Take?

_____

_____

_____

_____

_____

_____

_____

_____

My Notes

_____

_____

_____

_____

_____

_____

_____

_____

_____

_____

_____

_____

_____

Keep Learning

You will be the same person in five years but for two things: the BOOKS you read and the PEOPLE with whom you associate.
Mark Matteson

My late great mentor and publisher, Charlie "Tremendous" Jones, shared a version of that simple, yet profound quote twenty years ago. It changed my life. It's the title of my Podcast:

https://sparkingsuccess.net/category/podcast-episodes/

My learning is always aligned with my goals, a process that began when, at twelve years old, I was cut from the Madrona Junior High Basketball Team by Coach Kim Wilson. At first I was devastated. I walked up to the roster of players who had made the team, posted publicly in the boys' locker room. My name wasn't on it. My face turned red, first with embarrassment, then with anger. As I walked away, my emotions shifted to something deep inside me, an overwhelming desire to prove that coach wrong. It's something hardwired into my DNA. My father had it, I have it, my boys have it. *"You think I'm not good enough? I will show you!"*

The next day, I asked the best player at our school, Ken Christensen, whom I didn't really know that well, "How did you get so good?" He smiled at me with a surprised look. "No one ever asked me that before," he replied gratefully. "I shoot two hours a day, every day, and attend Bob Houbregs Basketball Camp on Whidbey Island in the summer."

Considering his reply, I asked, "Can you bring me the information on the camp?"

"You bet," he said. True to his word, he brought the brochure the next day (I still have it). That night I informed my father, "I've got to go to this camp . . ."

My father looked at it, smiled, tilted his head back, and replied with a measured but loving response, "It's not until next July? $110 huh? Well, if YOU earn half the money, your mother and I will pay the other half."

I was twelve. (I thought he was teaching me self-reliance. The truth was, we were poor!) I mowed lawns, washed windows, picked up debris, going around the neighborhood offering up my services. Over the next few months, I earned sixty bucks! At the camp the next summer, I met coaches and counselors who would change my life and inspire me to practice smart and hard. I made the team the next year. The roster was posted on November nineteenth, my thirteenth birthday. It was the best gift I've ever earned! That camp gave me valuable game experience and knowing what to practice in those two hours.

I also grew nine inches, which didn't hurt! But I made the team because I did many other things as well. I paid the price in advance.

1. I read every <u>article</u> in the sports page about basketball (still do)!
2. I read every <u>magazine</u> I could find on basketball.
3. I read every <u>book</u> I could find on basketball. (Do you remember "The Bookmobile?")
4. I <u>watched</u> every college "Game of the Week" on TV. (Yes, there was just ONE Game a week back then!)
5. I <u>played up</u> against older players every chance I got. I asked them for advice and ideas on how to improve my game.

6. I went to an open gym four to five nights a week and <u>played for hours</u>.

7. I set a <u>goal</u> to start by the end of the season. I started the last game of the season. That inspired me to set goals well into the future.

8. I attended my first <u>seminar</u> at fourteen years of age. It was a two-day event at Seattle University where I learned about goal achievement, visualization, self-esteem, managing my input: G.I.G.O = Garbage In, Garbage Out, meaning I must control my thoughts and emotions, monitoring what I allow in.

9. I <u>played</u> one-on-one with any guy who was older, taller, better than me, every chance I got.

10. I <u>dreamed</u> about playing basketball in college and set that as a Big Goal . . . and I eventually did.

11. I <u>listened</u> to games on my little transistor radio. I never missed a game.

12. I dribbled my basketball to school every day.

I tell my clients, let your learning be determined by your number-one goal. If you are in sales, read sales books. Ask the top salespeople in your industry how they got there. If you're a manager, read management books. Ask the top managers in your industry how they got there.

Charlie Jones hit the nail on the head: BOOKS AND PEOPLE. And yes, listen, think, dream, work, ask, go the extra mile. Keep learning.

> *Live as if you were to die tomorrow.*
> *Learn as if you were to live forever.*
> Mohandas Gandhi

> *The love of learning, the sequestered nooks,*
> *and all the sweet serenity of books.*
> Henry Wadsworth Longfellow

> *The more I read, the more I acquire,*
> *the more certain I am that I know nothing.*
> Voltaire

When was the last time you read a book in alignment with your goals?

Who can you reach out to who has done what you want to do and been where you want to go? Go find your Kenny Christensen. You might just make the team . . .

What One Action Will I Take?

_____
_____
_____
_____
_____
_____
_____
_____

My Notes

_____
_____
_____
_____
_____
_____
_____
_____
_____
_____
_____
_____
_____
_____
_____

Help Others

There is a time-tested aphorism in twelve-step programs
that expresses a great truth about the human condition:
"We don't get to keep something until we give it away."
It's really an oxymoron, like "Back up Forward" or
"Jumbo Shrimp." It's the Law of Compensation. Giving
always fosters abundance and reciprocity. What comes
back may not come from the receiver, but it always
comes back. Like gravity, it's a law. You might not
know about it, but it is. Ralph Waldo Emerson, in his
essay, "Compensation," wrote that each person is com-
pensated in like manner for that which he or she has con-
tributed. The Law of Compensation is another restate-
ment of the Law of Sowing and Reaping.

Come on, that's in the Bible! We reap what we sow,
positive or negative.

It's really saying YES and finding a way to increase
the quality and the quantity of our service to others. Our
income is in direct proportion to our service. *"We will
receive not what we idly wish for but what we justly
earn. Our rewards will always be in exact proportion to*

our service." My late great mentor Earl Nightingale taught me that.

It's really an attitude, a philosophy. *"Our attitude towards life determines life's attitude towards us. A bad attitude is like a flat tire. You can't go anywhere until you change it. There is no limit on earnings. The mind moves in the direction of our current dominant thoughts. Each of us creates his or her own life largely by our attitude."*

I learned a long time ago that I can be happy if someone gives me a gift. However, I can be equally happy if I GIVE someone a gift. You see, there is no limit on my happiness. If it's to be, it's up to me. I want to give without a thought to what I will receive in return. I must stop keeping score.

We are really talking about servant leadership. It's the Book of Luke.

What follows are ten simple things anyone can do to enrich their life and the lives of others.

1. Listen. Actively Listen to those you have the privilege of serving. Most people are simply waiting to talk. We have two ears, one mouth. We should listen twice as much as we talk.

2. Look for little ways to help others. I like to help little old ladies on airplanes get their bag down from the overhead. Hey, I'm six-foot-seven!

3. Let someone get into your lane on the freeway, even if they don't acknowledge it.

4. Hold the door for others, especially children and the elderly.

5. Smile. It takes thirteen facial muscles to smile, forty-seven to frown. Evidently, some people don't mind the extra work.

6. Say what you see. If someone is kind, say so. If someone looks great, tell them. If someone does well, affirm it. Become a *good finder.*

7. Offer your time to a worthy cause. Volunteer.

8. Look for ways to add value in unexpected ways. Stay a little longer, show up earlier, offer to help set up or tear down.

9. Bring flowers for the host of a dinner party.

10. Write a hand-written note or postcard and affirm on paper what you admire about that person. It will change their life and yours.

Folks who never do any more than they are paid for, never get paid for more than they do.
Elbert Hubbard

What can you do to increase the quality and quantity of your service to others today?

What One Action Will I Take?

_____

_____

_____

_____

_____

_____

_____

_____

My Notes

_____

_____

_____

_____

_____

_____

_____

_____

_____

_____

_____

_____

_____

Give Thanks

I try hard to hold fast to the truth that a full and thankful heart cannot entertain great conceits. When brimming with gratitude, one's heartbeat must surely result in outgoing love, the finest emotion that we can ever know.
Bill Wilson

The science of psychoneuroimmunology, introduced to a wider audience by Norman Cousins through his 1979 bestseller *Anatomy of an Illness*, proves to us that gratitude affects our health (www.Semel.UCLA.edu/cousins). The Norman Cousins Center for Psychoneuroimmunology at UCLA investigates the interactions between the brain and the body, the role of psychological well-being for health and recovery from illness, and the translation of such knowledge into effective behavioral strategies that prevent disease, promote healing, and enhance well-being across a lifespan.

Positive emotions strengthen our immune system, which enables us to resist disease and recover more quickly from illness. Gratitude, optimism, kindness, and laughter all serve to release endorphins into the bloodstream. Endorphins are the body's natural pain-killers that stimulate dilation of the blood vessels, which leads to a relaxed heart. Conversely, negative emotions such as worry, anger, resentment, fear, self-pity, and hopelessness slow down the movement of disease-fighting white cells and contribute to the development of stroke and heart disease by dumping high levels of adrenaline into the bloodstream.

In other words, FEAR kills, FAITH heals. We all need *Freedom from Fear* (which, coincidentally, is the title of my first book, available at:www.SparkingSuccess.net/bookstore).

I am a true believer. Why? Years ago, I was at death's door. Three days after my surgery in 2007 (I had a foot of my colon removed), I was not processing food. I was rushed back to the hospital a second time and the doctors removed my appendix and more of my colon. I should have died twice. During my recovery, I read up on this science of healing. I have made it a point to give thanks every day, aloud and on paper. I also made it a point to laugh every day. Moreover, I am on a mission to make other people laugh every day as well. *Laugh, Love, Learn, Leverage,* and *Leave a Legacy.* Those five

---

L's represent my life's purpose. I have made the time every day since 2007 to live those five L's, my L-5.

You cannot be grateful and unhappy at the same time.

Bestselling Author Melody Beattie wrote, *Gratitude unlocks the fullness of life. It turns what we have into enough, and more. It turns denial into acceptance, chaos into order, and confusion to clarity . . . Gratitude makes sense of our past, brings peace for today, and creates a vision for tomorrow.*

There are certain laws that operate whether or not we are aware of them. They are timeless laws, immutable principles that just are. Gratitude is one of those mysterious laws. The more gratitude we have, the more abundance we receive. The more cynical and ungrateful we are, the less we get. By becoming grateful, we set in motion a kind of magnet, attracting people, emotions, and attitudes that foster abundance. I don't completely understand it, but hey, I don't understand why my wife likes cut flowers. I buy them; they eventually die and are thrown away. However, I understand the effect. "Oh!" she exclaims. So I keep buying them. Gratitude is like that. When you combine gratitude with a positive expectancy, something magical happens: You become an "Inverse Paranoid." That is, someone who feels strongly that the world is out to do him or her good! Great things just start happening. Great people show up in your life. Great days become the norm. So how do I foster an "Attitude of Gratitude"?

Begin by making a "Gratitude List." What are ten things (or people) for which (or for whom) you are grateful? Make your list now:

1. _____

2. _____

3. _____

4. _____

5. _____

6. _____

7. _____

8. _____

9. _____

10. _____

11. _____

12. _____

When you find yourself having a tough day, grab a pen and paper and make a list. What makes you smile? What is great about your life right now? You see, it's impossible to be in the light and darkness at the same time. They cannot coexist. When you focus on what you are grateful for, pessimism, cynicism, and negative attitudes disappear. You are transformed. I have made hundreds of these lists over the last thirty years. They truly are magical. Optimism will sneak up on you in the process. Guess what? Optimists live longer than pessimists do. Moreover, they have a better time along the way. Ironic, isn't it?

So there it is. My simple philosophy of life. The six things I try every day to become . . .

Work Smart. Be Kind. Have Fun. Keep Learning. Help Others. Give Thanks.

How about you? What is your philosophy? I'd love to hear from you . . .

What One Action Will I Take?

_____

_____

_____

_____

_____

_____

_____

_____

My Notes

_____

_____

_____

_____

_____

_____

_____

_____

_____

_____

_____

_____

_____

_____

— Sixteen —

"Um, ya know, and um, like..."

A wise man speaks because he has something to say;
a fool speaks because he has to say something.
Plato

Everyone is in sales. Does that word make you un-
comfortable? Okay, how about influence? Everyone is in the influence business. We get one chance to
make a great first impression.

I recently had a teleconference with a young woman
who was trying to sell me her services. As I asked her
hard questions ("What does that mean to me?" and "Can
you provide me with three names of people that have
used your services?") she began to use "Um" in every
sentence. She said it three times in a row in one

sentence. Is "Um" even a word? What does it mean? According to Webster's Dictionary, it means, *"A word used to express doubt or uncertainty or to fill a pause when hesitating in speaking,"* and *"A representation of a common sound made when hesitating in speech."*

We all know people who use these bridge words or phrases. *"Um," "Ya know," "And uh," "Like..."* I don't know about you, but when I hear these annoying sounds, it's like fingernails on a chalkboard. One fellow I know said *"Ya know"* twenty-nine times in a five-minute talk. Yes, I was counting. It drove me to distraction. After a time, it's all I heard. His message was lost in a sea of *"Ya know"!* It shattered my confidence in him. I refer to him as *Ya Know Joe.* Of course, there are also *Ursula Umm, Angus and Uh,* and *Like Larry.* It holds them back from advancing in their career, like an emergency brake that's on when you are trying to drive fast. What to do?

Twenty years ago, I stumbled on a book in a used bookstore entitled *Write Better, Speak Better* by Readers Digest. It's a little 727-page hard cover tome. I devoured it. It covered:

1) How to use your voice

2) How to speak better

3) How to write better

4) Tools of the trade

It was, quite simply, a revelation. Might I remind you, I flunked high school English! This book redeemed me. It was the foundation upon which I built my business of speaking and writing.

As I thought of the things I have done over the last thirty years, I determined there were seven specific things I had done to change how I write and speak. I hope they help you make a better first impression and sell more of your product or service:

1. Develop a burning desire to improve your communication skills. All meaningful achievement begins with desire or inspirational dissatisfaction. What do you need to STOP doing? (What is, like, holding you back? Ummm . . .)

2. What do you need to START doing? Learn the value of what you offer. What are the reasons your product or service is of value to your prospects? Learn the benefits of what you sell. The Six Magic

Words of Influence are "What That Means to <u>Them</u> Is . . ."

3.   Ask a friend or peer to monitor your speech and writing for a few weeks. Record a five-minute talk and ask yourself, "What bridge words or phrases am I using that create doubt or uncertainty in my listeners?" Count them.

4.   Expand your vocabulary. Twenty years ago in invested in an audio program called *Vocab* by Bergen Evans. I learned five hundred new words in thirty days. I began reading the *New York Times* every Sunday. When I would hear or read a word I didn't know, I would look it up and write down the meaning, reviewing those words weekly until I could use each one in a sentence. *Succinct, anathema, deplorable, rigorous, cacophony, aberration, polyglot, misanthrope, magnanimous, benediction.* How many of these ten words do you know? Earl Nightingale taught me, "Your vocabulary is the one thing you cannot hide except by silence."

5.   Silence is golden. It's okay not to fill up every second with sounds. Sting contends that "It's the silence between the notes that makes the music."

When a comedian pauses, it is the audience's job to laugh. Comedy is a dialogue.

6. Attend Toastmasters on a weekly basis for a year. It's a group of committed business people who want to improve their speaking skills, vocabulary, and presentation skills. It's a loving, caring environment that offers a plethora of resources. They will help you eliminate your bridge words, *ya know,* without you noticing you have changed!

7. Slow down. It's not a race. Be deliberate in your delivery. Use commas in your speech. Think twice, speak once. Smile. Wait. Deliver. Watch one of President Obama's speeches. He is a master of the pause.

Each of us has one chance to make a great first impression. Have you seen the 2010 version of *True Grit* with Jeff Bridges? The fourteen-year-old protagonist is a young girl from Arkansas with great determination, an extensive vocabulary, and courage. She will not be denied. Her vocabulary belies her age. Adults take her seriously. Matt Damon's character, who starts by belittling her, eventually comes to respect her and says as much later in the film.

If you commit to these seven ideas for the next ninety days you will, like, grow, um, increase your income, and, uh, make a great first impression, ya know? people will want to spend time with you . . . no, really!

What One Action Will I Take?

_____

_____

_____

_____

_____

_____

_____

My Notes

_____

_____

_____

_____

_____

_____

_____

_____

_____

_____

_____

_____

— Seventeen —

A List of Lists

Learn to work harder on yourself than you do on your job. If you work hard on your job you can make a living, but if you work hard on yourself you'll make a fortune.
Jim Rohn

I **first heard the above quote in 1994** when Jim Rohn spoke in Seattle. I sat in the front row and took dozens of pages of notes. After the event, I stood in line and invested four hundred dollars, purchasing everything he had. I spent a year poring over his books, videos, and audio programs. It quite simply changed my life and income.

A coaching client of mine recently asked me how he could increase his self-confidence. He doubted himself.

These challenging times have tested us all on many levels, emotionally, physically, spiritually, inter-personally, financially. I explained that it was vital, if he was going to transcend turbulent times, to work on himself. I gave him some homework. I called it *My List of Lists!* Now I am sharing it with you. It's a list of exercises to be completed in your journal.

The List of Lists

❑ *WINS? (Make a list of past WINS going back to age five!)*

❑ *Five Goals to Achieve This Year = Write out the what and the why*

❑ *Hour of Power = <u>Read</u> Books about your number-one goal, <u>think</u> about the goal daily, <u>plan</u> your day on paper and prioritize*

❑ *Strength Bombardment = Soar with your strengths and increase your self-worth! (What is the best and highest use of your time?)*

❑ *Gimme Five, Man! = Attitude of gratitude habit (List what you are grateful for. A list of all your blessings!)*

❑ *I Like Me Because . . . (List the things about yourself that you are proud of)*

❑ *What's Great About <u>YOUR</u> Company, Products, and Services?*

❑ *Joy List (What activities bring you the most joy?)*

❑ *Resentment List (Learn to forgive and forget the past!)*

❑ *Who Am I? (List as many positive things about yourself you can think of)*

❑ *I Am Most Happy When . . . (Self-explanatory)*

❑ *Best Business Lesson Ever?*

❑ *Five Things I am Worried About List*

❑ *The Two Questions to Ask Your Children or Grandchildren at Night: What was the most fun you had today? What do you look forward to tomorrow?*

❑ *I Feel Most Appreciated When . . .*

The answers will change your perspective, attitude, beliefs, and infuse a measure of self-confidence that few people ever attain. How do I know? I have answered these questions many times. They represent the height of mental management.

Mr. Rohn passed away in 2009, but his legacy lives on. It turns out he was really on to something. If you work hard on yourself, you will not just change yourself, you will inspire others to change by your able example.

My children don't listen to word I say, but they watch every move I make! My guess is that your children do, too! I've got some work to do . . .

What One Action Will I Take?

_____

_____

_____

_____

_____

_____

_____

My Notes

_____

_____

_____

_____

_____

_____

_____

_____

_____

_____

_____

_____

_____

—Eighteen—

My Real Clients Are . . .

*If you bungle raising your children,
I don't think whatever else you do matters very much.*
Jackie Kennedy

Boy (and girl), how true that is. As parents, we do the best job we can at that moment in time based on our awareness and experience. I know I was a better dad with our youngest simply because I had some experience. When our first and oldest son, Colin, was two, when he fell down, as two-year-olds do, we would be right there and ask, "Are you okay?" This often made things worse, not better. It was almost as if we were saying, "You should be scared, *we* are!" When Evan came along, if he fell we would say, "You are fine. Get up."

Why? Because he WAS fine. We didn't give him a cue to cry. It made him tougher. *Awareness and experience.*

A few years ago, I was presenting to five hundred people at a large conference in Cleveland, Ohio. I said, *"You know, you are not my real clients. My real clients are your children and grandchildren! What I am about to share is for them. You are simply the voice to communicate these timeless and proven principles to raise successful and well-adjusted children, both at home and at work. Your employees are just BIG KIDS!"*

When our boys were young, my wife read a book by Zig Ziglar. She shared a passage with me:

> *Raising children today is a tough job, but it is the most rewarding, fulfilling job you can have. The best thing you can learn is that if you instill in your children character-building and moral values as early in their lives as possible, the rewards your family reaps will be something you'll treasure later on.*

So what exactly can new parents do to "Raise Positive Children in a Negative World?" (By the way, these ten principles apply to employees equally well).

Ten Habits to Raise Healthy, Happy, High-Functioning Adults

1. Make certain you and your spouse are on the same page. A consistent message is vital. Divide and conquer will sabotage your parental efforts.

2. "Affirm" to your children "Your future is so bright it burns my eyes . . ." again and again. Plant the seed of a bright future for them.

3. Reward the behavior you want repeated. Whatever gets rewarded gets repeated. It's the greatest management principle in the world.

4. Praise progress, effort, and the grind. Say, "Good. Now try it again." It's the key to raising children who understand we have to earn what we have.

5. Show them how to deserve your time. When our oldest asked me to rebound for him, I replied, "If you READ any of these books for an hour, I will rebound for you for an hour." It worked. He read fifteen of the finest self-help books over the next six months, books that I had read in my forties!

6. Affirm the belief, "In this family, we finish what we start. We don't quit!"

7. When they do fall down, drop the ball, or lose the game, plant the seed of faith by saying things like, "You'll get them next time!" or "You got this!" or "I'm proud of your effort, you gave it your best. That's all that matters."

8. Lead by able example. My children never listened to a word I said but they watched every move I made. When my words and actions are aligned, the message gets through. Remember *the Window and the Mirror:* When it's time to take the credit, look out the window and give it away. When it's time to take the blame, look in the mirror.

9. Make certain they know that you are PROUD of them and that you LOVE them. You can never say that often enough, no matter how old they are.

10. Teach them to forgive their enemies and let go of resentment. "Resentment is like taking poison and expecting the other person to die."

Despite the overwhelming adversity Jackie Kennedy experienced in her lifetime, she did a great job of raising her children. She was right, "If you bungle raising your children, I don't think whatever else you do matters very much."

Why not give some of these ideas a try with your children and employees?

After all, they are my *real* clients.

What One Action Will I Take?

_____

_____

_____

_____

_____

_____

_____

My Notes

_____

_____

_____

_____

_____

_____

_____

_____

_____

_____

_____

_____

_____

—Nineteen—

Anchors Away!

You gotta stop watering dead plants. We teach people how to treat us. It's so nice when toxic people stop talking to you. It's like the trash took itself out. You cannot always change the people around you, but you can change the people you choose to be around.
Mark Matteson

In my sixty-four years on Earth I have concluded that there are two kinds of people: Anchors and Speedboats. Anchors pull us down; Speedboats pull us forward.

Which one are you?

You will be the same person you are today in five years but for two things: The <u>Books</u> You Read and the <u>People</u> With Whom You Associate!
Mark Matteson

Speedboats are easy to spot. They are kind, loving, generous, humble, honest, caring, gentle, strong, and have a positive attitude. They have a gift for getting along with others. By their words and actions, they tell us they are here to help us and build us up. Like firefighters, they walk in when others walk out. They say things like, *"Good for you, you earned it!"* or *"Way to go, that's awesome!"* or *"I'm so proud of your efforts and progress!"* They lift us up. They are quite simply *heroes* and *sheroes*. They are GOOD-finders.

Anchors are a little trickier to spot. They are sneaky, manipulative, dishonest, narcissistic, and crafty. They are cowards. They try to make us feel less-than. In order to spot them, we have to define them. Here are some clues:

1. **Blame-Throwers.** "Who broke this coffee cup?" Their motto is, "When at first you don't succeed, blame someone quickly!" They take zero accountability and responsibility for their

actions and decisions. They point fingers at others. They never look inward concerning their words and behavior. They engage in negative and passive-aggressive behavior. Sometimes they engage in "gaslighting," whereby they point out your faults and attempt to make you feel small and unworthy, as if all of their problems were your fault.

2. **Peter or Paula Pessimist.** They are downers. They see the glass as half empty. If the weatherperson says there's a ten percent chance of rain, they focus on that instead of the ninety percent chance of sun. Their focus is on what is wrong with you, the economy, the government, different generations, the world in general. They believe bad things are permanent and will never change and that they have no control over their futures. They believe that good things won't last. It's exhausting being around them. They spread viral misery.

3. **H.R.C.K.I.A.** = **H**elp-**R**ejecting **C**omplainers **W**ho **K**now **I**t **A**ll. When they complain and you offer a solution, they dismiss it. They don't want help, they just want to complain. They search for sympathy and people of similar ilk instead of

remedies. They talk incessantly about their bad health, injuries, sickness, or lack of success. When you suggest an idea that has worked for you, they say, "That wouldn't work for me . . ." or "I'm not like you . . ." or "My parents never gave me . . ." They choose to stay stuck in their own stories. They refuse any attempt to edit their own story, or change their attitude or behavior in any positive way.

4. **Dogmatic Dudes (and Dudettes)** This group offers opinions or beliefs as *facts*. They, too, remain stuck in their story and fixed in their opinions. Their dogma ran over their Karma! Similar to Know-It-Alls, they seek and find other people to validate their beliefs. They are unteachable, arrogant, and unwilling to listen to any other side. They say things like, "I know that . . ." or "According to Fox News . . ." or "According to CNN . . ." (Constant Negative News!).

5. **Billy or Barbara Braggart.** False humility or outright bragging about their accomplishments is the order of the day. They talk way too much about themselves and their accomplishments (real or imagined). They rarely if ever listen to others. The lack any kind of empathy and

concern. Often trying to one-up others by saying things like, "This one time, at band camp . . ." or "That's nothing, five years ago, when I was climbing Mt. Rainier . . ."

When you come across these "Little Hitlers" sometimes the best thing to do is smile and walk away. It's not always feasible, though, as some of them are co-workers or, worse, relatives. Trying to help them or change their behavior is futile, so ask yourself, "How can I limit my time with them?"

The following five books helped me to understand and deal with these Anchors:

1. *Nasty People,* by Jay Carter
2. *Your Perfect Right,* by Robert Alberti and Michael Emmons
3. *How to Win Friends and Influence People,* by Dale Carnegie
4. *The Power of Good News,* by Hal Urban
5. *Learned Optimism,* by Martin Seligman

Here are a few simple things anyone can do when you find yourself in the company of Anchors:

128

1. Smile and nod
2. Paraphrase their emotions ("You feel frustrated . . ." or "You feel strongly about that . . .")
3. Ask "What CAN you do? What is OUT OF YOUR CONTROL?"
4. If they choose to stay stuck, limit your time with them as much as possible.
5. If they continue to try to engage you in their misery, assert yourself and simply say, "Sorry but I can't do this right now. I've got to go."
6. Stop replying to their phone calls, texts, or emails (It's called "Gracious Ghosting").
7. Find some new friends with whom to associate.

Life is too short to invest your precious time with people who try to drag you down. Anchors Away! Go find some new friends who pull you forward. Speedboats please!

Anchors or Speedboats? Who will you choose to spend time with? You decide. Five years is a short period of time . . .

With whom do you associate and why?

What One Action Will I Take?

_____

_____

_____

_____

_____

_____

_____

_____

My Notes

_____

_____

_____

_____

_____

_____

_____

_____

_____

_____

_____

_____

_____

—Twenty—

Pluck a Thistle and Plant a Rose

A fellow is just about as happy as he
makes his mind up to be.
Abraham Lincoln

A client recently asked me how I wanted to be re-membered after I'm gone. Pausing for effect, I smiled and said, "I want people to say that I plucked a thistle and planted a rose where I thought it would grow!" It's a quote from Abraham Lincoln. He should know. He experienced more adversity in twenty years that than a hundred men do in a lifetime. He lost three of his four children. He was married to a women who was described by others as a "wildcat" and a "she-devil" and a "shrew". She was arguably the meanest, most self-centered person ever to live in the White House. He lost his mother, Nancy Hanks Lincoln, the only woman he ever truly loved, Ann Rutledge, at an early age. He grew up poor. He suffered from deep depression most of his life and, of course, he was assassinated in 1865 at the age of fifty-six. It's a long list. So why is he considered the greatest president this country has ever seen?

Here is the famous list of Lincoln's failures. Don't think you have any chance of being successful? Based on his past record of failures, Abraham Lincoln had no right to think he could win the presidency of the United States. But that didn't keep him from trying. Consider this:

Abraham Lincoln . . .

Failed in business at age 21.

Was defeated in a legislative race at age 22.

Failed again in business at age 24.

Overcame the death of his sweetheart at age 26.

Had a nervous breakdown at age 27.

Lost a congressional race at age 34.

Lost a congressional race at age 36.

Lost a senatorial race at age 45.

Failed in an effort to become vice-president at age 47.

Lost a senatorial race at age 47.
Was elected PRESIDENT at age 52!

Positive Opposites. Thistles to Roses.

What follows are Ten Positive Opposites. Abe understood the human condition. He made others feel important. What if you focused on one positive habit each month like Honest Abe did? You can't enjoy the rose without the thorns.

1. Complain? Appreciate!
2. Lie? Be honest!
3. Tear others down? Build others up!
4. Ignore people? Greet people with enthusiasm and use their names!
5. Gossip? Praise!
6. Blame Others? Accept 100% responsibility!
7. Talk about yourself? Ask about others!
8. Be sarcastic? Be sincere and laugh at yourself!
9. Talk too much? Listen actively!
10. Avoid eye contact? Smile and make eye contact!

When you adopt these positive opposites, and make them a habitual part of who and how you are, you will attract more friends, influence others in positive ways, and enjoy long-term and healthy relationships. Moreover, you will pass these traits on to your children and grandchildren.

Good habits are hard to form, but easy to live with. These ten habits will change your life in ways that will astound you. I am still working on making them a consistent way of being for myself.

Four score and seven years ago our fathers brought forth on this continent, a new nation, conceived in Liberty, and dedicated to the proposition that all men are created equal . . .

The world will little note, nor long remember what we say here, but it can never forget what they did here. It is for us the living, rather, to be dedicated here to the unfinished work which they who fought here have thus far so nobly advanced. It is rather for us to be here dedicated to the great task remaining before us—that from these honored dead we take increased devotion to that cause for which they gave the last full measure of devotion— that we here highly resolve that these dead shall not have died in vain—that this nation, under God, shall have a new birth of freedom— and that government of the people, by the people, for the people, shall not perish from the earth.

Abraham Lincoln
November 19, 1863

Look over there! A thistle. Now where can I find some roses?

What One Action Will I Take?

_____

_____

_____

_____

_____

_____

_____

My Notes

_____

_____

_____

_____

_____

_____

_____

_____

_____

_____

_____

_____

—Twenty-One—

A.N.T.s at Your Picnic?

You **might not have heard of John Burroughs.** He was an American essayist and naturalist who lived and wrote after the manner of Henry David Thoreau, studying and celebrating nature. *"I go to nature to be soothed and healed, and to have my senses put in order."* He was friends with John Muir, Henry Ford, Tom Edison, Luther Burbank, and Teddy Roosevelt.

From various retreats, he wrote for half a century on nature subjects. His later writings showed a more philosophic mood and a greater disposition toward literary or meditative *allusion* than did his earlier work. My favorite quotes from this brilliant man include:

Leap, and the net will appear.

A man can fail many times, but he isn't a failure until he begins to blame somebody else.

How beautifully leaves grow old. How full of light and color are their last days.

The lure of the distant and the difficult is deceptive. The great opportunity is where you are.

A somebody was once a nobody who wanted to and did!

The smallest deed is better than the greatest intention.

Did you know that each of us has over sixty thousand thoughts a day and, according to UCLA's Brain Institute, fully seventy-five percent of those thoughts are negative? Why is that? There are many factors that influence our thinking and beliefs to forge our self-talk: social media, books, movies, music, the news, it's a long list. All of our input helps to form our self-talk.

Self-talk? What's that?

It's our automatic thoughts that come in three categories:

1. Silent thoughts unspoken
2. Thoughts we say aloud to ourselves
3. Thoughts we say aloud to others

One of my favorite quotes is, *"Remain silent and risk appearing the fool, speak and remove all doubt."*

One of the most interesting ways to get in touch with your self-talk is while driving your car or golfing. What do you say to yourself when someone cuts you off then gives you "half-a-peace-sign"? Or when you put your first shot off the tee into the sand trap or water hazard? What you say, either silently or aloud, tells you a great deal about how effective your mental management abilities and overall health are.

Beware of the **A.N.T.**s at your picnic! Automatic Negative Thoughts.

Dr. Daniel Amen in his extraordinary book, *Change Your Brain, Change Your Life,* came home one night after a particularly bad day at the office dealing with suicide risks, angst-ridden teens, and dysfunctional couples to find thousands of ants in his kitchen. "It was gross," he wrote. "As I started to clean them up, the acronym came to me. I thought of my patients from that day— like my infested kitchen, my patients' brains were infested by negative thoughts that were robbing them of their joy and stealing their happiness. The next day, I brought a can of ant spray to work as a visual aid and have been working diligently ever since to help my pattens eradicate their **A.N.T.**s!"

If you argue for your limitations you get to keep them, like an attorney in a courtroom. First, we form habits—then our habits form us. A.N.T.s are just a habit of thinking. We can change them. What follows is my formula for improving self-talk and killing A.N.T.s:

1. Listen closely to the self-talk of others and ask yourself, are they positive or negative? (Why is it easier to take other people's inventory than it is your own?)
2. Pay attention to what you think to yourself, especially when you win or when you lose (or when driving).
3. Listen to the words you say aloud, get in touch with your automatic thoughts.

4. Challenge them with authority using the turna-round phrase, "Up until now . . ."

5. Then say, "Next time I intend to . . ."

6. Write them down and examine the impact. Do they help or hurt?

7. Resolve to improve your thinking with positive opposites.

The best example of positive opposites is the St. Francis Prayer:

God, Make me an instrument of your peace. Where there is hatred, let me sow LOVE;

Where there is injury, PARDON;

Where there is doubt, FAITH;

Where there is despair, HOPE;

Where there is darkness, LIGHT;

Where there is sadness, JOY.

Grant that I may not so much seek to be consoled as TO CONSOLE;

To be understood, as TO UNDERSTAND;

To be loved as TO LOVE;

For it is in GIVING that we receive;

It is in PARDONING that we are pardoned;

It is in DYING, that we are born to eternal life.

Have you gotten in touch with your negative self-talk? A.N.T.s sound like this:

"What's the matter with me anyway?"

"If it wasn't for bad luck, I wouldn't have any luck at all!"

"The world is against me! I never get a break."

"That son of a gun cut me off. I'll show him!"

The list goes on and on. Self-talk is tricky business. It takes a while to change old habits. We all talk to ourselves. Again, it falls into three categories:

1. **SILENT self-talk.** The things we say to ourselves in our heads.

2. **PERSONAL self-talk.** The things we say aloud to ourselves.

3. **PUBLIC self-talk.** The reactive things we say to others.

I have found that certain emotions, especially resentment, self-pity, anger, and fear manifest all manner of strange, unhealthy, negative outbursts. When I write down the things I say, patterns emerge, certain key words come up over and over again, like: "TRY" "SHOULD" "MUST" "HAVE TO." They all conspire to drag me down or hold me back. Writing them down really helps me quiet the chatter, and get in touch with negative habitual words that hurt me and others. What do you say to yourself?

I suspect John Burroughs had many picnics and some A.N.T.s tried to spoil them. Did he live to be eighty-four years young because he learned how to deal with A.N.T.s? I'd like to think so. For me, I aspire to add years to my life and life to my years. That means bringing my A.N.T. spray to the office every day!

How about you? How Is Your SELF-TALK?

What One Action Will I Take?

_____

_____

_____

_____

_____

_____

_____

_____

My Notes

_____

_____

_____

_____

_____

_____

_____

_____

_____

_____

_____

_____

_____

—Twenty-Two—

Goals? Thanks, Earl!

I **started this book** with advice from Earl Nightingale: *"We Become What We THINK About!"* It truly is the Strangest Secret in the World. Over the years, thirty of them to be exact, Earl inspired me to offer the following advice in all my seminars. It has changed my life and the lives of many of my seminar attendees.

> *I want you to write on a card what it is you want more than anything else . . . Think about it in a cheerful, relaxed, positive way each morning when you get up, and immediately you have something to work for—something to get out of bed for, something to live for. Look at it every chance you get during the day and just before going to bed at night. As you look at it, remember that you must become what you think about, and*

*since you're thinking about your goal, you real-
ize that soon it will be yours . . . It is yours for the
asking.*

First we work on goals, then they work on us. This
is not new information, In fact, The Old Testament says,
"Without a vision, the people perish." You see, the moment you decide on a goal to work toward, you are immediately successful. You are then in that rare and successful category of people who know where they are going.

Out of every hundred people, you belong to the top
five. Don't concern yourself too much with how you are
going to achieve your goal. Leave that completely to a
power greater than yourself. All you have to do is know
where you are going. The answers will come to you of
their own accord.

Goals add years to our lives, and life to our years. It
gives our lives meaning and purpose. 68% of American
men in this country are dead within eighteen and
twenty-four months of retirement. Why is that? Nothing
to look forward to! Men derive meaning from work.
(Evidently women have other things to give them

meaning, like grandchildren and friends. They are so much healthier than men.)

One of my favorite stories was also a favorite of the late President John F. Kennedy. It goes like this:

A wise old farmer asked his fourteen-year-old grandson to help him with a long overdue project: to remove the boards from a six-foot-high fence. He laid out exactly WHAT he wanted done and WHY it was so important, as any good leader would. The HOW was up to his grandson.

He checked back on his grandson an hour later only to find the young man standing there wearing his favorite cowboy hat staring at the imposing task. Not a single board had been removed. "What's wrong, Johnny?" the grandfather asked.

Looking down at his cowboy boots in shame, Johnny replied, "Well, this fence is so high and it's going to take a lot of work and time for me to get all the boards down. I am having a hard time getting started." He tipped his favorite hat back on his young head in frustration.

The farmer grabbed his grandson's cowboy hat and threw it over the fence.

"Hey, why did you do that? That's my favorite hat!"

"As I told your father when he was your age, in order to get your hat back, you are going to have to take down a few boards. Once you get going, you might find you have to take down a few more. At that point, you may decide to stop for the day. That's okay because you can come back tomorrow, throw your hat over the fence again and take down a few more boards. Eventually, before you know it, the job is done."

Wanting is not enough. We need to take action! All of us need something to look forward to. Goals give us just that.

In her extraordinary 2016 book, *Grit,* Angela Duckworth describes Warren Buffett's simple "3-Step Goal Achievement Process."

1. *Write at least twenty-five career goals in your journal.*
2. *Circle the five highest-priority goals.*
3. *Take a good hard look at the twenty you did NOT circle.*

What are your five top goals?

1._____
2._____
3._____
4._____
5._____

Discipline is the bridge between goals
and accomplishment.
Jim Rohn

Remember Earl's advice: ***"WE BECOME WHAT WE THINK ABOUT!"***

There you have it. What will you THINK about over the next five years? That is a very short amount of time in what is, for most people, a long life.

Where is your focus?

I'd love to hear your thoughts. Feel free to reach out to me. I promise to listen.

What One Action Will I Take?

_____

_____

_____

_____

_____

_____

_____

_____

My Notes

_____

_____

_____

_____

_____

_____

_____

_____

_____

_____

_____

_____

_____

_____

About Mark Matteson

Mark Matteson is an international speaker and the author of the bestselling book *Freedom from Fear* which has sold over 200,000 copies worldwide. He has written six books and ten eBooks. He is one of those rare professionals who can say he is speaker, consultant, podcaster, publisher, and author and *mean* it. He has attracted clients like Microsoft, Honda, Fujitsu, Daikin, Mitsubishi, T-Mobile, John Deere, Conoco-Phillips, Aflac, Honeywell, and other Fortune-100 companies on three continents. He has been called "an edu-tainer," "an oracle of optimism," "a superlative street scholar," and "an intense idea-reporter." Mark travels 250 days a year around the globe, delivering seventy-five key-notes, seminars, and workshops a year. He is a gifted sto-ryteller, using self-effacing humor, high levels of interac-tion, and powerful and proven business principles to in-spire audiences to the highest levels of productivity and profit. Mark leaves audiences wanting more.

Mark began his career in HVAC in 1976. He has been married to Debbie for forty-two years and has three grown sons and three grandchildren.

He takes great pride in the fact that he once flunked high scool English!

Mark Matteson
Bestselling Author, International Speaker

To order one of my books, go to
www.SparkingSuccess.net/store

Phone: 206.697.0454

To subscribe to Mark's monthly ezine, go to
Mark@SparkingSuccess.net

To watch a few short videos,
visit https://tinyurl.com/8e7udabj

To Listen to my Podcasts, visit:

Google Play: https://tinyurl.com/5n5b5ydn

Apple: https://tinyurl.com/4zvvyy

"Make it a great day . . . unless you have other plans!"